Cotswold
Villages

Cotswold Villages

Photographs by Rob Talbot

WEIDENFELD AND NICOLSON
LONDON

Introduction

*L*imestone cottages, sturdy manors and farms, glorious gardens, rolling hills and idyllic villages – these have attracted people to the Cotswolds for years. The area became fashionable in the 1880s, after being 'discovered' by William Morris and the Arts and Crafts movement and has remained popular ever since. Before the improved transportation networks, the villages of the Cotswolds were not well known to the outside world, despite their ancient history. Sometimes referred to as the capital of the Cotswolds, Cirencester was an important trading and administrative centre in Roman times; its name derives from the Roman *Corinium*. It was

the Middle Ages, however, that saw the real rise in prosperity of the region as the hills became home to the thousands of sheep that provided the market for England's international wool trade. The unusually high proportion of well-built village houses were the homes of successful merchants, while the stone barns standing among the hills are the legacy not so much of sheltering the sheep but of keeping the valuable fleeces secure from thieves.

Yet it is perhaps their geological formation that gives the Cotswolds their character. Stretching from the Avon north of Bristol and north Wiltshire, across a large section of eastern Gloucestershire and the north-west part of Oxfordshire, the range of mellow hills reaches a maximum height of slightly over a thousand feet at Cleeve Hill in Gloucestershire. The composition of the hills, however, is what lends the villages their distinct flavour; most of the buildings were constructed with locally quarried rock. Usually honey coloured or grey, the stones give each village a satisfying unity.

Today, the Cotswolds offer something for everyone. Whether in the magnificent Perpendicular-style 'wool churches', the artistic communities where artisans continue the traditions of their fore-bears, or the footpaths that wind through the picturesque country-side, the villages of the Cotswolds are a glorious testament to England's rich rural history.

LITTLE BARRINGTON

*T*HE charm of each cottage in this village is enhanced by their sublte difference from each other. In the seventeenth century, the quarrying of the area's limestone brought the village wealth and useful building material.

BISLEY

*N*ARROW walkways meander through
this town, distinguished by a series of at-
tractive, beautifully maintained gardens.
Hemmed in by cottages, Wesley House has
architectural features dating from the sixteenth
through to the eighteenth centuries.

SNOWSHILL

*T*HIS village has ancient roots, and its geo-
graphical position keeps it from the hands of
modern intervention. The honey-coloured
stone cottages have maintained their timeless
appeal, despite the weathering of the years.

BOURTON-ON-THE-WATER

*C*ROSSING the Windrush river, these low bridges are a characteristic feature of the village. There are traces of ancient settlements here, and several museums featuring local traditions make this scenic location a popular attraction.

FAIRFORD

WATCHING over the Coln river is the Perpendicular church of St Mary, adorned with a superb display of sculptures and painted-glass windows. Many of Fairford's seventeenth- and eighteenth-century houses, like this riverside mill house, remain.

STANTON

*A*FTER being brought back to life early this century by a far-sighted and wealthy architect, this small village in the northern Cotswolds contains much of architectural interest, such as its manor farm fashioned out of old cottages and a host of stone dwellings.

PAINSWICK

*T*HE Flemish weavers who settled in this village left a glorious legacy of grey-stone buildings. One of Painswick's most intriguing sights is the churchyard of St Mary's, which has the areas's finest collection of table tombs.

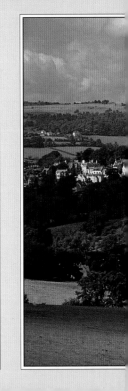

NAUNTON

*N*ESTLING along the Windrush river, this small village has expanded over the centuries. From a cluster of buildings Naunton evolved to a more linear configuration bordering the river. The parish church of St Andrew (left) is mainly sixteenth century.

BIBURY

*P*OPULARIZED by William Morris, this enchanting village has a fascinating Saxon past, the legacy of which can be seen in its church. The long Arlington Row, with its steeply gabled cottages and seventeenth-century interiors, and a trout farm that makes use of the picturesque stream, are open to the public.

WINCHCOMBE

*T*HIS old market town still has vestiges of its former importance, exhibited today in the village's museums. A casual stroll around the village reveals unexpected pleasures, like this narrow street of grey-stone cottages.

HILLESLEY

ONLY five miles from the magnificent estate of Badminton, owned by the Duke of Beaufort, lies this tiny unassuming village surrounded by hunting country. The fine barn is a feature typical of the Cotswolds, although many have been converted to dwellings.

BROADWAY

◆

*A*T an important crossroads in Hereford and Worcester, this is one of the most beautiful and most popular villages in the Cotswolds. Broadway boasts a fine high street with stone houses from the sixteenth to the eighteenth centuries.

BROADWAY

❖

*T*HE limestone houses of Broadway's high street exude a sense of history. There is a manor house in which as the fortunes of war shifted, both Charles II and Oliver Cromwell stayed on separate occasions. Also on the street, which leads up to Fish Hill and its panoramic views, is the famous Lygon Arms Hotel.

TETBURY

A SMALL hillside market town with roots in the thirteenth century, Tetbury plays host to a large number of visitors each year. Plunging down its hill are the Chipping steps, flanked by lovely cottages dating back to medieval times.

MINCHINHAMPTON

A PRODUCT of flourishing wool and cloth trades, Minchinhampton is a compact village of grey-stone buildings, the focus of which is the unusual *c.* 1700 market house, which is supported by stone pillars.

CIRENCESTER

*O*NE of the principal Roman towns of the
first century AD, Cirencester, like many
Cotswold villages, became increasingly important with the wool trade in the Middle Ages.
Excavations have uncovered some of the
Roman foundations, and many relics from the
period can be seen today.

WINDRUSH

*B*ORDERING a triangular village green are
several cottages of stone quarried from the
hill onto which they are grafted. A number of
other barns and houses in Windrush date back
to the eighteenth and nineteenth centuries.

HIDCOTE BARTRIM

*C*LOSE to the outstanding gardens of Hidcote Manor, a late-seventeenth-century house that was somewhat altered in the eighteenth century, lies a tiny village that comprises little more than a few thatched cottages.

CASTLE COMBE

A SAXON castle on a nearby hill is this village's namesake. Cottages lies on either side of the By Brook. The sixteenth-century manor house, now a hotel, thirteenth-century market cross, and a church with a range of Gothic details are a reminder of Castle Combe's former prosperity.

ILMINGTON

*H*OME to a splendid Norman parish church, St Mary's, this lovely village at the northern end of the Cotswolds is set in a delightful position overlooking the Stour valley. Its relative isolation has given rise to a number of local legends.

DONNINGTON

A DAMMED river gracefully abuts a village that still has a number of seventeenth- and eighteenth-century cottages constructed in the traditional style of the area. Beside the lake is a brewery whose intriguing buildings form the centrepiece of the village.

Chipping Campden

*T*HE village's wool-trading significance in the Middle Ages is still evident in such buildings as the fourteenth-century town hall and seventeenth-century market hall. Here, on the high street, are stone houses that reflect the affluence of the families of that era.

CHIPPING CAMPDEN

*A*BOVE a blanket of snow rises the parish church of St James, built primarily in the fifteenth century. The loftiness of its Perpendicular-style tower is a telling symbol of the prosperity the village once enjoyed.

SNOWSHILL

ERCHED on the side of a veritable hill of snow, this secluded village remains much as it was centuries ago. The cottages are not arrayed in any order, just placed where the earth would support them.

ACKNOWLEDGEMENTS

Copyright © George Weidenfeld and Nicolson 1994
Photographs © Talbot-Whiteman

First published in Great Britain in 1994 by George Weidenfeld and Nicolson Ltd
Orion House, 5 Upper St Martin's Lane, London WC2H 9EA

British Library Cataloguing-in-Publication Data
A catalogue record for this book is available from the British Library

Cover and series design by Peter Bridgewater/Bridgewater Book Company
Series Editor: Lucas Dietrich

The photographic material in this book has appeared in the Country Series volume
The Cotswolds by Robin Whiteman and Rob Talbot.